Territories of the United States

GUAM

Jill Keppeler

PowerKiDS press

Published in 2025 by The Rosen Publishing Group, Inc.
2544 Clinton Street, Buffalo, NY 14224

First Edition

Editor: Therese Shea
Book Design: Rachel Rising

Photo Credits:Cover J nel/Shutterstock.com; Cover, 1, 3-32 boromvit tatasai/Shutterstock.com; Cover, 1, 3-32 P-fotography/Shutterstock.com; Cover, 1, 7, 11, 13, 15, 17, 19, 23, 29 https://ch.m.wikipedia.org/wiki/Litratu:Flag_of_Guam.svg; p. 4 em_concepts/Shutterstock.com; p. 5 Peter Hermes Furian/Shutterstock.com; p. 5 Rainer Lesniewski/Shutterstock.com;p. 7 https://en.m.wikipedia.org/wiki/File:Guam_ali_2011364_lrg.jpg; p. 8 Conceptual Art/Shutterstock.com; p. 9 Eric Celebrezze/Shutterstock.com; p. 11 https://en.m.wikipedia.org/wiki/File:Hagatna_from_Fort_Santa_Agueda.JPG; p. 13 Randy Davis/Shutterstock.com; p. 15 es3n/Shutterstock.com; p. 17 Everett Collection/Shutterstock.com; p. 19 https://en.wikipedia.org/wiki/File:James_Moylan_official_photo.jpg; p. 20 Bubble Beanie/Shutterstock.com; p. 21 Sasa Huzjak / Alamy Stock Photo; p. 22 JAYSPICK/Shutterstock.com; p. 23 https://commons.wikimedia.org/wiki/File:Guam%27s_72nd_Liberation_Day_Parade_140114-F-LP948-161.jpg; p. 24 Millenius/Shutterstock.com; p. 25 https://commons.wikimedia.org/wiki/File:President_Donald_J._Trump_Meets_with_Governors-Elect_(32440544868).jpg; p. 26 androver/Shutterstock.com; p. 27 https://commons.wikimedia.org/wiki/File:Sailors_say_the_Pledge_of_Allegiance_with_Guam_elementary_students._(15669571832).jpg; p. 28 Wirestock Creators/Shutterstock.com.

Library of Congress Cataloging-in-Publication Data

Names: Keppeler, Jill, author.
Title: Guam / Jill Keppeler.
Description: [Buffalo, New York] : PowerKids Press, 2025. | Series: Territories of the United States | Includes bibliographical references and index.
Identifiers: LCCN 2024004151 (print) | LCCN 2024004152 (ebook) | ISBN 9781725329072 (library binding) | ISBN 9781725329058 (paperback) | ISBN 9781725329089 (ebook)
Subjects: LCSH: Guam--Juvenile literature.
Classification: LCC DU647 .K477 2025 (print) | LCC DU647 (ebook) | DDC 996.7--dc23/eng/20240216
LC record available at https://lccn.loc.gov/2024004151
LC ebook record available at https://lccn.loc.gov/2024004152

Manufactured in the United States of America

CONTENTS

Westernmost

Out in the western Pacific Ocean, in the region called Micronesia and the archipelago, or island group, called the Mariana Islands, is an island of about 210 square miles (544 sq km). It's far smaller than any U.S. state (Rhode Island is 1,214 square miles [3,144 sq km]) and even than many U.S. cities, but it's home to more than 169,000 U.S. citizens. This island, Guam, is a territory of the United States and the westernmost point of the country.

Guam has a long history and a flourishing blend of **cultures**. Much of the population is of the native Chamorro people. Many U.S. soldiers are stationed there, as the island's location is important to national security, or safety. Military and tourism are two major parts of the territory's economy.

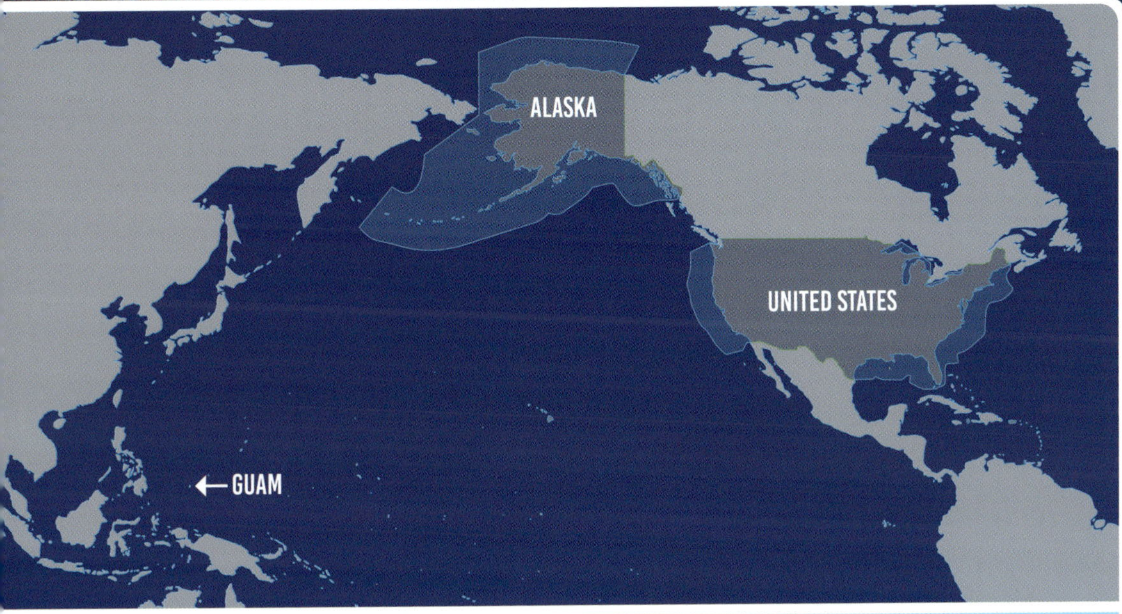

Guam is about three times the area of Washington, D.C. Hawaii is the closest state, about 3,960 miles (6,373 km) away.

Part of the Marianas

Guam is the biggest and most southern of the Mariana Islands. This chain of islands was formed by volcanic eruptions millions of years ago. The islands are the tops of a huge underwater mountain range that starts at the bottom of the Mariana Trench, a wide, deep cut in the ocean floor. The southern Marianas are older than the northern islands. Some are still active volcanoes.

Guam shares the archipelago with another U.S. territory, the **Commonwealth** of the Northern Mariana Islands (CNMI). The CNMI includes the islands of Saipan, Tinian, and Rota. Its islands extend about 450 miles (724 km) from the north of Guam. The two territories have separate governments even though they're close neighbors. Rota, to the north, is Guam's closest neighbor. The Federated States of Micronesia is to the south.

Territorial Truths ☆☆☆☆☆

Udall Point in Guam is the westernmost point in the territory, so it's considered the westernmost point of the United States. Point Udall in the U.S. Virgin Islands is the easternmost point. They were named for brothers!

THE DEEPEST DEPTHS

The Mariana Trench is one of the most mysterious places on Earth. It's nearly 7 miles (11.3 km) deep and is the deepest known part of Earth. In fact, it's deeper than Mount Everest is tall. (Everest is Earth's highest mountain above sea level.) The Mariana Trench was named a U.S. national monument in 2009. People haven't been able to explore the depths much because of the huge amount of pressure that far under the ocean's surface.

Guam is about 30 miles (48.3 km) long from northeast to southwest. You can see two military airstrips on this image.

A Tropical Island

Guam has a tropical climate. This means that it's warm and wet, with temperatures between about 70 and 90 degrees Fahrenheit (about 21 and 32°C). While northeast **trade winds** moderate this a little, these temperatures don't change much throughout the year. There's about 95 inches (241 cm) of rain each year, most of which falls during the wet season from about July to December.

Guam's even climate makes it popular for tourists. However, it also has typhoons, called hurricanes in other parts of the world, which are large, circular storms that form over warm ocean waters. After typhoons caused a lot of damage in Guam in the 1960s, people started building many structures with concrete instead of traditional building materials, such as wood. Cement is often used today.

Territorial Truths ☆☆☆☆☆

The island sometimes experiences earthquakes, which can be followed by the huge ocean waves (or series of waves) called tsunamis. Both can cause a lot of damage.

Typhoon Mawar hit Guam in May 2023. U.S. president Joe Biden declared Guam a major disaster area because of the damage.

Nineteen Villages

Guam's capital is Hagåtña, formerly called Agana. It's a town of about 1,000 people on the island's west coast. Today, it's one of the smallest villages, although it used to be one of the largest. It existed before European colonizers arrived in the Marianas, though little is known about it. However, it's also considered one of the first European cities in the Pacific, from the late 17th century.

There are no cities in Guam. There are 19 main municipalities called villages. Dededo, in the north, has the largest population with about 42,900 people, while Yigo is the largest in land size, about 35 square miles (91 sq km). Each city has an elected mayor, and these mayors (and their vice mayors) make up the Mayor's Council of Guam.

Territorial Truths ☆☆☆☆☆

The name "Agana" was officially changed to Hagåtña in 1998. The new name comes from the word for blood in the Chamorro language of Guam.

MILITARY LAND

About one-third of the land in Guam is owned and controlled by the U.S. military. Andersen Air Force Base is in the village of Yigo in the northern end of Guam. This base, created in the 1940s, is home to about 8,000 service members, family members, and others. Naval Base Guam is in the south of the island, in the village of Sånta Rita-Sumai. Thousands more naval personnel and sailors live there.

Hagåtña is small, but it's also one of the island's main commercial, or business, districts.

Flowers, Fruit Bats, and More

Guam has many tropical plants, including palm trees, flowers, and flowerless plants called ferns. The bougainvillea, or paper flower, is the territorial flower. There are many kinds of animals as well, including insects and marine animals. Wildlife species include coconut crabs, the Mariana fruit bat, the Mariana monitor lizard, and the cane toad. Though there are many wild chickens, other native species of birds have struggled to survive in the wild in recent years.

There have been many issues with **invasive species** in Guam. Most notable is the case of the brown tree snake, which arrived by cargo ship during World War II (1939–1945). These snakes have greatly harmed local bird species. Island authorities have been working for years to get rid of this pest.

Territorial Truths ☆☆☆☆☆

Another common animal in Guam is the carabao, or water buffalo. People originally brought them to the island to help with farming during the Spanish colonization.

AN INVASIVE ISSUE

The brown tree snake has caused many birds of Guam to become extinct in the wild, including two species not naturally found anywhere else in the world: the Guam rail and the Guam flycatcher. (The Guam rail was saved from total extinction by being bred in cages.) Brown tree snakes also hunt other small creatures, and they've caused power outages by damaging equipment. They have no native predators to keep them in check.

The Mariana monitor lizard is called the *hilitai* in the Chamorro language. They can be up to 3 feet (0.9 m) long.

Colonization and War

Indonesian-Filipino people of Southeast Asia first settled in Guam about 1500 BCE. These people became the Chamorro people of today's Mariana Islands. In 1521, however, explorer Ferdinand Magellan was the first European to find the island, and by 1565, Spain had claimed it. The country was used as a resupplying stop for ships. In the late 1600s, Spain officially colonized Guam. The Chamorro people had to deal with both cruel colonizers and the diseases they brought with them. The population on the Mariana Islands fell from perhaps as many as 100,000 people to about 1,000 by 1820.

The Spanish-American War of 1898 changed things again. When Spain lost this war, it ceded, or gave, Guam (as well as the Philippines and Puerto Rico) to the United States. A string of U.S. naval officers governed the island, denying local rule.

Territorial Truths ☆☆☆☆☆

The United States captured Guam on June 21, 1898, during the Spanish-American War. The USS *Charleston* took part in this capture, but there was no bloodshed.

BEFORE SPAIN

The people of Guam had an established society well before Spain arrived. They built *latte* houses, which were homes set on top of stone columns, and many swift types of canoes. They grew rice, made pottery, and did a lot of fishing for food. The society was matrilineal, or traced descent through women. People were divided into different **castes**. Those in the upper caste were generally on the coasts, and the lower were inland.

Latte pillars, which used to support rectangular houses, are still scattered throughout Guam and the Marianas. They're a symbol of the Chamorro people.

Occupied

In 1941, after the start of World War II, the clash of world powers rattled this small island again. After the Japanese attacked Pearl Harbor in Hawaii on December 7, 1941, the Japanese landed on Guam, which is far closer to Japan than any other part of the United States. They took over the island within days, starting a nearly three-year **occupation**. During this time, the Japanese treated the Chamorro people horribly. They were forced to work long, hard hours for the Japanese and, toward the end of the war, held in **concentration camps**. Many were beaten, tortured, or executed. More than 1,100 people died.

On August 10, 1944, after weeks of fighting, **Allied** forces retook Guam, destroying the two largest villages, including Hagåtña. The people of Guam were free of Japan, but the island was badly damaged.

Territorial Truths

After the Allies retook Guam, the U.S. military took large amounts of land for its increased presence there. This displaced many Chamorro families from their homes, and they were often not repaid.

THE RESISTANCE

The Chamorro people resisted the Japanese during the occupation. They quietly (and sometimes not as quietly) worked against the invaders, including concealing and protecting George Tweed, a U.S. serviceman who'd escaped capture by the Japanese. One noted hero of this time was Father Jesus Baza Duenas, a Chamorro Catholic priest. Duenas stood up against many injustices from the Japanese. When they suspected him of knowing Tweed's whereabouts, the Japanese tortured and then killed him.

This photo shows an airstrip on the Orote **Peninsula** in Guam, recaptured by U.S. Marines in 1944.

Becoming a Territory

After the war, the Chamorro people of Guam still had to fight for their rights, as the control of the island returned to the U.S. naval governors. Guam's leaders persisted in the fight for self-government, however, and in 1950, the U.S. Congress passed the Organic Act of Guam. This made residents of Guam, including the Chamorro, citizens of the United States and established the island as an official unincorporated U.S. territory. The U.S. president appointed civilian, or nonmilitary, governors.

Over the years, Guam has begun to move toward more self-government. U.S. president Dwight Eisenhower appointed Joseph Flores, the first governor from the Chamorro people, in 1960. In 1970, Guam's people chose the first popularly elected governor, Carlos Camacho. In 1973, Guam began to have one nonvoting delegate in the U.S. House of Representatives.

Territorial Truths ☆☆☆☆☆

Guam has the right to create a territorial constitution, but despite two constitutional **conventions**, the island's voters have not approved one. Guam's citizens have also considered becoming a commonwealth.

WHAT IS A TERRITORY?

There are five major territories of the United States. In addition to Guam, these are Puerto Rico, the U.S. Virgin Islands, the Commonwealth of the Northern Mariana Islands, and American Samoa. The residents of four of these territories are citizens. (American Samoans are **nationals**, not citizens.) All pay some federal taxes, but they can't vote for the U.S. presidents and only have some self-government. These territories are unincorporated, which means that only certain parts of the U.S. Constitution apply to them, unlike for U.S. states.

As of early 2024, Guam's representative in the U.S. House of Representatives is James Moylan, shown. He can't vote on passing laws but does get a vote in congressional committees.

Håfa Adai!

Today, more than 32 percent of the people of Guam call themselves Chamorro. Some Chamorro have other ancestries as well, including Spanish and Filipino. About 30 percent of the population are Filipino. A smaller percentage hail from Micronesian islands, such as the Chuukese, Palauans, and Pohnpeians. About 7 percent identify as white. South Korea, China, and Japan are also represented. The large military population adds more **diversity**.

English and Chamorro are both official languages of Guam. Many people also speak Filipino languages, with scatterings of other Pacific island and Asian languages. Schools and businesses tend to use English, while people speak Chamorro at home. The Chamorro language today has many Spanish words, and other languages such as Japanese and English have also influenced it.

Territorial Truths ☆☆☆☆☆

As fewer young people today speak the Chamorro language, some people in Guam are working to increase education, including creating the island's first Chamorro school.

The usual greeting in the Chamorro language is "*Håfa adai!*" It means something like, "What's up?" or "Hello!"

Diverse Culture

The culture of Guam reflects its diversity. Many Chamorro customs continue, now mixed with some traditions of Spanish and mainland American culture. After years of Spanish colonization, most people are Roman Catholic, and Catholic churches are often the center of village events, including fiestas. The villages each have a patron saint whose feast day is celebrated each year with food. Music and singing, both modern and traditional, are popular.

People still practice the traditional arts of Guam, including weaving and carving. Gef Pa'go Chamorro Cultural Village is a community in the village of Inalåhan. There, some of the Chamorro people demonstrate, or show, their traditional arts and other practices, including cooking, to visitors. In Hagåtña, the Guam Museum hosts many exhibits about the island's history and culture.

COCONUT JUICE

TASTY TRADITIONS

One notable aspect of Guam's culture is its traditional foods. These have been influenced by many different groups and ingredients from the island. Coconut is a common ingredient, as are rice, bananas, and taro, a root vegetable. Chamorro barbecue is meat seasoned with soy sauce, vinegar, lemon, sugar, and other seasonings and then grilled. Other popular staples include red rice, which has been soaked with achote, or annatto, seeds, and the spicy sauce called *fina'denne'.*

For the most part, Guam celebrates the same holidays as the rest of the United States. One additional holiday (and perhaps the biggest) is Liberation Day, celebrated on July 21, which remembers when the island was liberated, or freed, from the Japanese during World War II.

Three Branches

As of early 2024, Guam is still governed under the 1950 Organic Act of Guam. However, a 1968 amendment, or change in the act, allowed for the election of a governor who serves a four-year term. Everyone 18 and older can vote. The Mayors' Council of Guam makes recommendations to the rest of the government. Like the U.S. federal government, Guam's government has three branches: executive (governor, lieutenant governor, and appointed cabinet), legislative (an elected 15-member legislature), and judicial (a Guam Supreme Court, district court, and local courts).

While Guam has a nonvoting representative in the U.S. Congress and its people can't vote for the U.S. president, it does have some influence. For example, it sends delegates to the national Democratic and Republican conventions, who help select candidates for U.S. president.

Territorial Truths ☆☆☆☆☆

As of early 2024, Lourdes Leon Guerrero is the governor of Guam and has been since 2019. She's a former nurse and the first woman to be governor of Guam.

Guam governor Lourdes Leon Guerrero meets with the U.S. president and others at the White House.

Industry and Education

Much of Guam's economy relies on the military bases and the tourism industry. The COVID-19 **pandemic** damaged its tourism, and it still hasn't fully bounced back. There were only about 40 percent of the tourism arrivals in 2023 that there were before COVID-19. While there are still agricultural businesses in Guam, the island imports most of its food now. Many Guamanians used to farm and fish for a living but now work at the bases or in tourism.

As in the rest of the United States, education in Guam is required from about the ages of 6 to 16. The island has one school district with about 40 schools of different levels. Beyond that, colleges include the University of Guam, Guam Community College, and Pacific Islands University.

Territorial Truths ☆☆☆☆☆

Many of the tourists who visit Guam are from Japan. The island used to get more than 1 million tourists a year but fell far short of that in 2023.

School in Guam is much like school anywhere else in the United States. Students read, write, play, and learn math and science.

The Future

Guam's unique, or one-of-a-kind, position in the Pacific can be a cause for worry for its military and civilian residents. In recent years, North Korea has threatened the small island (only about 2,100 miles [3,380 km] away) with attack. The United States stores weapons and military equipment such as bombers in Guam. In early 2024, North Korea claimed to be testing new missiles, or rockets, that can reach the island. In return, the United States has been further fortifying, or strengthening, the region.

Another big question for the island's future is the question of its status with the United States. Many of Guam's people expressed interest in becoming a commonwealth or a state, while others want independence. Only time will tell what's next for this little island with a big history.

TIMELINE

AROUND 1500 BCE — People from Southeast Asia first settle in Guam.

1521 — Explorer Ferdinand Magellan first arrives at the island.

1565 — Spain claims Guam and uses it as a resupply stop for ships.

LATE 1600s — Spain officially colonizes Guam.

1898 — The Spanish-American War takes place. Spain cedes Guam to the United States. The U.S. Navy takes over the island.

DECEMBER 1941 — The Japanese land on Guam after attacking Pearl Harbor. This is the start of a nearly three-year occupation.

AUGUST 10, 1944 — After weeks of fighting, Allied forces retake Guam.

1950 — U.S. Congress passes the Organic Act of Guam, making the people of Guam citizens of the United States and making the island an official unincorporated U.S. territory.

1960 — Joseph Flores, the first governor from the Chamorro people, is appointed.

1970 — Guam's people choose the first elected governor, Carlos Camacho.

2017 — North Korea threatens to attack Guam.

Glossary

Allied: Having to do with the group of nations, including England and the United States, in World War II that opposed the Axis nations, including Germany and Japan.

caste: A grouping of society based on differences of rank or wealth.

commonwealth: A territory that has political or economic connections with another country.

concentration camp: A kind of prison during a war where people who aren't soldiers are kept and forced to live and work in bad conditions.

convention: A gathering of people who have a common interest or purpose.

culture: The beliefs and ways of life of a group of people.

diversity: The quality or state of having many different types, forms, or ideas.

invasive species: A kind of living thing likely to spread and do harm when placed in a new area.

occupation: The holding and control of an area by a foreign military force.

national: Someone under the protection of a nation without having the status of citizen.

pandemic: A time or event in which a disease spreads quickly and affects a large number of people in a wide area or around the world.

peninsula: A narrow piece of land that extends into water from the mainland.

trade wind: An ongoing wind that blows toward the equator.

For More Information

Books

Black, Riley. *Deep Water: From the Frilled Shark to the Dumbo Octopus and From the Continental Shelf to the Mariana Trench.* London, England: Welbeck, 2023.

Mack, Doug. *The Not-Quite States of America.* New York, NY: W. W. Norton & Company, 2018.

Mooney, Carla. *Historic Battles from World War II for Kids: 15 Battles from Europe and the Pacific.* Emeryville, CA: Rockridge Press, 2022.

Websites

Ducksters: Guam
www.ducksters.com/geography/country.php?country=Guam
Ducksters offers links and facts about this U.S. territory.

Håfa Adai!
www.visitguam.com
Learn more about this territory from the Guam Visitors Bureau.

National Geographic Kids: Guam
kids.nationalgeographic.com/geography/u-s-states-and-territories/article/guam
National Geographic Kids presents more about Guam.

INDEX